Positive Thoughts
for Daily
Meditation

Positive Thoughts
for Daily
Meditation

ELEMENT
Shaftesbury, Dorset ● Rockport, Massachusetts
Brisbane, Queensland

© The Sivathondan Society 1993

Published in Great Britain in 1993 by
Element Books Limited
Longmead, Shaftesbury, Dorset

Published in the USA in 1993 by
Element, Inc
42 Broadway, Rockport, MA 01966

Published in Australia in 1993 by
Element Books Limited for
Jacaranda Wiley Limited
33 Park Road, Milton, Brisbane, 4064

Cover design by Max Fairbrother
Design by Nancy Lawrence
Typeset by Phil Payter Graphics, Southsea, Hants.
Printed and bound in Great Britain by
Redwood Books, Trowbridge, Wiltshire

British Library Cataloguing in Publication
data available

Library of Congress Cataloging in Publication
data available

ISBN 1-85230-426-X

Introduction

The fundamental aim of all religions is the realization of truth. This is a matter of direct experience, in which neither the mind nor the intellect nor any human faculty is involved. It is a question of being.

Those who have attained this state are exceedingly rare. But one such 'realized soul', known to his followers as Yogaswami, lived in Jaffna in North Sri Lanka for over ninety years and left his body there in 1964.

The contents of this book are some of his sayings, taken from the note-books of four of his followers, who made it a practice of writing them down immediately after each meeting with him.

He was born in 1872 and received his early education in a Christian missionary school where, although not christened, he was given the name John. Later he was known as 'Johnswami', which came to be corrupted to 'Johanswami' and then 'Yogaswami'.

Nearly all his devotees were householders and engaged in some employment or other. He rarely advised them to retire from active life. People would often come and say that they wanted to give up their jobs in order to be able to devote more time to spiritual practices; but he did not usually encourage them to do this, since, for him, the whole of a person's life had to be made a spiritual practice, and he would not admit any division of human activity into 'holy' and 'unholy'. To most of those who came to him he would end by saying, 'Now, go and do your work.' He laid great emphasis on work, and 'work for work's sake' was, like meditation or God or what is real, one of the 'medicines' that he most frequently administered.

Since most of his followers were Hindus, his teaching was usually expressed in Hindu terms. But he himself was beyond all distinctions of religion and would address visitors in language that they could understand. Buddhists, Christians, Muslims and agnostics would all come to him for help and guidance, because he had reached the summit to which philosophies and religions are merely paths.

The Sayings

'In the beginning was the Word and the Word was with God and the Word was God.' That is the basis of all religions.

God will tell us everything.
Let us not worry about anything.

You must remain like the mariner's compass.

You are your own friend
and your own enemy.

Happiness and sorrow are twins.
Let them come and go like the clouds.

Do not allow the mind to run in different directions. You must make it become one-pointed.

Learn to remain always happy.

You must have the capacity to endure everything.

There is one thing God cannot do —
He cannot separate Himself from the soul.

You lack nothing.
The only thing you lack is that you
do not know who you are.

Let us improve ourselves instead of
trying to improve the world.

Whatever work you have to do,
do it well.

All work must be done with the aim
of reaching God.

You must work, but you must not worry
about it after it is finished.

Without being content with what you have,
you will always want more
and therefore suffer.

Everything will turn out successfully when
the mind is not agitated.

Wisdom will come if you do your work well.

If the chimney is full of smoke,
how can the light be seen?
If the mind is full of dirt,
how can the soul shine?

How foolish it is to judge someone
by one bad quality, ignoring all their other
good qualities.

More often than not I think I am
in the presence of God. This is a good way
to remain pure.

Provided we don't think of flying in the air,
we can attain whatever we desire.

As one brings up one's children well,
so one must train the mind to behave well.

Do not think that if such and such a thing happens it is good; or if some other thing does not happen it is bad.

If you are a king,
will you have contentment?
If you are a beggar,
will you have contentment?
Whatever your walk in life may be,
you will only have contentment through knowing yourself by yourself.

Mind is our best friend and
our worst enemy.

We must improve ourselves. We should not
look to others for our own improvement.

Who can be a better friend to us than God?

Instead of thinking that we are all servants of God and that all is His action, we make resolves and plans and thus create a world within ourselves and suffer out of it.

❦

Acquiring more and more knowledge will only tend to diffuse your mind. Directing the mind inwards will give you peace.

*If you catch hold of the cat by its tail, it will
bite you. The world will do the same.
Live in the world like water on a lotus leaf.*

*What does a man lack if he surrenders
himself to the Lord with the conviction
that all is His action? He will get
everything he needs.*

If you press the switch there will be light.
God is in the heart of every one of us, like
the power-station generating electricity.

Why wander about saying:
'Don't drink! Don't commit adultery!
Don't do this and don't do that!'
Let God look after those things.
Who can improve the world?

Everyone must find out the path that suits them. The train can only run on rails.

Don't do things in order to please others.

We must demolish the fortress that we ourselves have built.

As we kiss our children every day
before going to work, so should we daily love
the Lord and do our work.

Don't run anyone down. That habit will
give you mental worry. Get rid of bad habits
as a result of experience. Beginning with the
excuse that it is only a medicine, people take
alcohol and then become drunkards.

*If we put into practice the little we know,
that is enough. We will come to know
everything in that way.*

*As a man at the helm of a ship attends to
other things while holding the rudder, yet
brings the ship safely to harbour, so the
desire for self-knowledge is enough. Like the
rudder, the desire for self-knowledge will
keep you on the right course and take you to
your goal. You don't need to worry about
acquiring 'this' or getting rid of 'that'.*

Instead of spending time in book-reading, it is better to spend it in studying yourself.

Do not worship God with the aim of obtaining some profit. Do not worship even with the desire for liberation.

Why do you want to open the outside door when there is an inside door? Everything is within.

If you try to stop the mind, it will only become more active. It is not necessary to stop it. You must ask it where it is going.

When you worship God, do not ask for anything. Worship for the sake of love. Afterwards you can ask for your requirements.

The grace of God is with everyone.

With one hand take hold of God,
with the other hold on to the world.

Speak what comes from within.
Otherwise don't speak.

If you worship God with the love of a child,
you will regain all that you have lost.

Even in small things, act with care and see everything in relation to everything else.

*All thought must die. Alas!
How difficult that is!*

Just as this farmer has prepared his soil well, so everyone must try to keep his heart pure.

All are His actions.

First obey; then command.

If you remove illusion, you will see that God pervades everything.

*One method is to stop all thought.
Another method is to remain simply as a
witness, allowing thoughts to come and go.
As one becomes more and more mature in
this practice, thoughts will begin to come
from the inner silence. Be very attentive to
those thoughts.*

*Do not allow the light to be blown out by the
wind. Lack of faith, doubt and worldly
desire — these are the wind.*

Be alone. Be alert.
Be like a fisherman watching his float.

Worldly attachment is the obstacle to
knowledge of truth.

It is not a question of analysing yourself.
It is a question of seeing yourself.

See everything you see as God.
Do everything you do as service of God.
Give up this 'me' and 'mine'.

God is within you. But we place Him
outside and worship Him.
Clever is the person who sees God both
inside and outside.

You are always in Him and He is always in you. You lack nothing.

Attachments tell on the body and mind, but nothing can affect the spirit.

He who does right need not fear anybody.

Let happiness and sorrow come and go like day and night. Don't fear!

❧

As an oil lamp shines, so all of you must light the lamp within you.

❧

The God within you will reveal to you everything that you need. There is no need to ask anything from others.

Man lives in God.

God and you are inseparable.

Wherever you look you see God. I was ruining myself by not realizing this.

The Lord is with all of us. Then why should we try to lord it over others?

When you have entirely surrendered, everything you do will be meditation.

Be yourself!
Stand on your own legs!

Take care of the body and let it engage itself in good action, but remain apart and let your mind dwell on God.

This world is a big temple to which all kinds of pilgrims come — good, bad and indifferent. Let us concentrate on our own worship and not find fault with what others do.

We should take a lesson from Mother Earth.
She treats alike both the good and the bad —
the snake and the tiger as well as
the cow and the goat.

Have faith and confidence in yourself. Let
your greater self guide you. Faith can do
wonders. Doubt is the greatest sin.

God is, God is not. At the top of the mountain there is nothing but God. At the foot of it there is all the manifold variety and conflict.

All life, all the elements, all the variety of existence — all are like the streams flowing from the mountain top. All the streams ultimately merge in the sea.

How do we know the will of God?
Sometimes it is clearly reflected in the mind.
Sometimes the words of the sages will reveal
it. And at other times it is not clear at all.

Meditate in the morning and evening and at
night before you go to bed. Sit quietly for
about two minutes. You will find everything
in your life falling into place and your
prayers answered.

Everything emanates from the great silence.
The world has been a playground of the
Lord from time immemorial.

The God within you will guide you.

Don't go halfway to meet difficulties.
Face them as they come to you.

The correct measure has been measured out to each one. This cannot be altered. You should realize this and do what comes naturally to you. Then you will be happy.

There is no need for hero-worship. The distinction between so-called 'great' and 'small' does not exist. All are various forms of the one reality.

Liberation is within you.

Be true to yourself.
Don't alter your behaviour simply to
please others.

Ill health is also a blessing.
The flesh and the ego are weakened and
contemplation of God becomes easier.

Joy and sorrow only exist in the mind.

Never act against your conscience out of fear of authority.

Look on praise and blame alike.

Knowledge gained from the company of
great souls is superior to book-knowledge.

The ornaments of the soul are justice,
integrity, courage and truth.

Bad men obey out of fear.
Good men obey out of love.

You cannot get rid of evil simply by exposing it. If you try to be good, loving and honest, evil will disappear.

He who has no patience cannot be a man of justice.

Learning means removing the veil of ignorance.

One who does good to others
does good to himself.

❦

You cannot improve others or the world.
Improve yourself.

❦

He who has strength of mind will not
be agitated. If you are agitated you
cannot know the truth.

You came into the world empty-handed.
And when the call comes you leave it
empty-handed.

Don't let your ego spoil the intellect given
you by God's grace.

Whether others treat you with kindness or
with rudeness, do not be affected.

That one is beautiful who,
though crippled in body,
is not crippled in mind.

❦

It is not a simple thing to control the mind.
It cannot be done in a day, or even in a
year. Through constant effort thoughts can
be controlled a little. In this way the
uncontrollable mind can finally be brought
under control. This is the supreme victory.

Be a student always.
And that is a most difficult thing to be.

The knowledge of God cannot be contained
within the limits of any book.

Waves rise in the ocean. So waves of
thought arise in the mind. The aim is to
control thoughts as they arise.

It does not matter what anybody says. It does not matter what holy books say. Consult your own experience and accept as true only what conforms to it.

The world is a training-ground for the achievement of freedom. Everyone does their part according to their own measure.

A jak-fruit is large in size but hangs by a slender stalk. In the same way, the whole world depends on an unknowable energy for all its activities. It is the same whether this is called 'God' or given any other name.

The whole universe is peaceful and silent. There is peace and silence in the midst of noise.

You can hear the voice of God in everything
and everyone.

God speaks through flowers as well as
through the tongues of men.

If you go on finding fault, you will lose all
your friends. The picture may be bad, but
why spit on it?

The wise will discard feelings of 'me' and 'mine'. Their aim will be spiritual advancement. They will transcend birth and death and will live at the feet of the Lord in perpetual bliss.

*There is nothing wanting in us.
Our only defect is the want of the realization of this truth.*

You must learn to be cool and calm.
Learn to be cool and calm in the midst of
intense activity.

Never be in a hurry. We keep away from
those in a hurry.

Detachment involves a great deal of effort.
Detachment gives you strength.

It is not a question of seeing God. How can the part see the whole? Regard everything as a manifestation of God. The servants of the Lord regard every single thing as the Lord Himself. They grow in that conviction and realize the truth.

It is only when you can take good care of precious things that they come to you. You must prepare the ground for them. That is the state of wealth.

Work for the sake of work. You cannot be without work. Look at the sun. Who knows when it came into being? It has always been there. Think of yourself as one who has always been there and do your work. It is all a glorious game. People call it the dance of the Lord.

Happiness and sorrow, honour and dishonour occur one after the other. Don't lose heart when you discover this. At the foot of the mountain you are aware of the high ground and the low ground. When you reach the top, the whole thing is just one beautiful spectacle.

*If you want to be free from suffering,
pray to God.*

*It is all one. Yet there are many names and
shapes and appearances.*

*Live a disciplined life. Everything else will
take care of itself.*

God exists. The world is at peace. God is peace. What happens on the surface is all a game. God is overwhelmingly present everywhere.

Think of the world as one. Let your thoughts embrace the whole. Do not give up prayers or formal worship — but go further and further. If you have set out for a destination you may enjoy what you see on the way, but you should not stop on the way.

Of what use is it to remain in deep meditation? Attain a state of permanent self-awareness at all times and in all places. Live with everybody, in the midst of everybody, but never forget your true self.

As food is necessary for life, so is prayer necessary for the realization of the truth. But prayer is an aid and not the end.

The present is the result of past action. Man is the architect of his future.

You will know Him if you keep quiet.

The world is by nature illusory.
Yet God is incessantly and indefatigably at work all the time.

Take good care of your body, if you want to attain divine wisdom. If you don't it will be very difficult indeed.

If an earthquake does you harm, do you try to harm it in return? We just keep quiet. Let everyone mind his own business.

Love is God. Truth is God. You cannot see God with your eyes; you must experience God. God is all things. God is everywhere.

Stand upright. Be disciplined. Be friendly.
You will lack nothing.

Running water will run faster if
you remove an obstruction here and there.
You need not do much more.

Why should a man work? That question
should not arise. Can you ask why God
exists? This is a similar question.

The hand does its work, the leg its work. So everyone does their work – the trees their work, the labourers their work. God is the great ruler who sits witnessing it all. There is nothing imperfect in the world. Witness everything as God does.

God speaks everywhere through everyone. Everywhere, all the time and in everyone you can hear the voice of God.

One truth exists. We cannot claim to have
seen it. We cannot say that we have not
seen it. It is an open secret. Sages have
appeared from time to time, said one thing
and another, then disappeared. Truth
remains itself, ever unknowable, ever new.

Once you have realized the truth
you can give up work if you want to.
But until you realize it you must go on
working. Sloth is the greatest danger.
There is no wisdom in work itself.
Wisdom lies in your attitude to work.

*Choose any system of enquiry and truth
manages to get lost in the system.*

*Don't surrender your liberty to anyone.
Don't be deceived because one man says one
thing and another says another thing.*

*It is wrong to kill a tiger in its forest. But
you must kill it if it enters the village.*

Discriminate between the permanent and the perishable. Make the discrimination certain and then do well any work that you choose to do.

Continue to work. While you work you may do right and you may then do wrong. But you must continue to work.

The heights of life are more difficult
to climb than the Himalayas.
How numerous are the obstructions!
Even towards the end the ego will
raise its head.

Don't think of anything as unnecessary and
don't think of anything as necessary either.
Continue to work.

It is not proper to give up work. Fight! The world is a battlefield. Accept anything that comes. Do not give up out of fear or pity.

Good thoughts and bad thoughts are twins.

The truth is one. The rest is illusion. Truth is betrayed by the first attempt at articulation.

You must realize the truth yourself.
No. It is wrong even to put it that way.
How can we express something changeless
and beyond the comprehension of the mind?
The whole is the truth.

It is not enough just to be harmless.
You must even be angry and assertive.
Of what use is it if other people merely call
you a good man?

There is order in the universe. The thief and the trouble-maker are part of this order.

What is in my heart is the same as what is in yours. That is what is everywhere.

There is always a reaction to every action. Meet situations simply, as they arise.

'God exists. He is everywhere. He is with me, and I have all I need.' This is what the wise ones tell us. I believe this and live in it. You do not need much learning. It is enough if you can live in the light of this.

You should not even think evil of other people. Don't even give a chance for other people to misunderstand you. The religious life is one in which you live in peace and happiness with everybody.

Live in the world like the man who runs
away from rain for fear of being drenched.
Live without colliding. Shake off delusions
and stand on your own self.

The turtle lays a thousand eggs and
remains silent. The hen lays just one egg and
cackles endlessly. Be like the turtle.
Don't behave like the hen.

Be a servant of the Lord within yourself. It does not matter how you appear outwardly.

❦

There is a wick within us.
You can light it if you want to.

❦

Who can live long enough to enjoy all the wealth he has accumulated? It is sufficient to have just enough to live on.

If you want to live without worry,
reduce your wants.

All great souls have undergone suffering.
None can escape what is ordained.

Do your duty as the sun and
the moon do theirs.

Nothing exists except the Lord.
Everything is His action.
Place all your burdens under
His holy feet and rest.
Don't give room for sorrow or despair.
Don't have regrets — 'I did this' or 'he did
that'. Be awake!

※

Understand that all those actions that arise
from the maya are a help to realize God.
By raising him up and bringing him down
again and again the Lord makes a man gain
experience. Get rid of all illusion.
All tests are for good.

*You must have desire and you must also
have the ego if you want to realize God.
How can you know God without the ego?*

*The usefulness of any action depends
a great deal on the attitude of mind of the
person who acts.*

*Be patient until you realize the truth
and can enjoy it.*

Do not see God in a particular place or particular way. God is in everything and beyond everything.

One in many; many in one.

You cannot see that which makes you see.

Be as a child.

Be in your place. Work in your place.

Work according to your capacity.
Ten gallons – ten gallons capacity.

Do not speak before you understand.

*Guard your tongue. Otherwise
harm will come to you.*

*Be like a crane which stands doing nothing,
but when it sees food it is immediately
alert and pounces at once.*

Don't be a pessimist.
Don't be an optimist.
Middle path.

Time is short. The subject is vast.

You cannot realize. I cannot realize.
There is no 'you', no 'I'.

You cannot know the truth. Get rid of that idea. Truth is. All is truth. Truth is 'I am'.

This idea of 'knowing' must be surrendered.

Surrender everything. 'I', 'you' and 'he' must be surrendered. You must go beyond.

You are climbing Everest. You must struggle — struggle the whole way. All the time struggle.

Go as you please – just play!
All is play. God is play.

Only you can work. Only you can do it.

Find the truth! Sit down till you find it!

You move up from truth to truth.

First hear; then enquire; then understand.

No need to say anything. Just be!
That is enough.

Nothing changes, but there is change.

Nothing is lost, nothing is gained. It is. Loss
and gain imply change. Change is illusion.

He who says he knows does not know.
Nobody knows.

Let your greater Self direct you.

If you don't know, you are pure. Not
knowing is purity. Then you are humble.
If you know, you are not pure.

Act, *but don't care for the fruits of action.*

Prayer is consciousness.

Nobody knows — I don't know. It is indescribable; it is inexpressible.

The mind must be absolutely still, like a lake with no ripples.

Do not be bound by anybody or anything. You must be free.

The whole world will look after you. If I am angry, I am looking after you.

Give to others — *without attachment.*
Help others, but without attachment.

If you give to others, do so with attention.

Don't follow me. Don't follow anyone.
Follow yourself.

Until you understand, you must be very
careful. Watch every step. Examine yourself
every day. That is the first step. First step,
second step, third step — and so on,
till you come to the top.

He who is in devoted pursuit of truth
endures hunger, thirst, fatigue and the harm
done by others.

Very easy to humbug.

❧

When you understand, you can do what you like. Dance!

❧

All is spirit-movement. All movement, all change is spirit-movement.

All are struggling to the top like corks in a bucket of water.

See God everywhere. This is practice. First do it intellectually. Then you will know it.

You don't want to see God. You must feel God. God is you. Just be that!

Act in the moment. Commands come from moment to moment — 'Go here!' 'Go there!'

What you think, that you become. If you think God, you become God. If you think food, you become food. Everything comes to you. Just worship God — order what you want! No need to know.

If you don't want anything,
everything comes. If you reject something,
that thing will come.

Say, 'O Lord, I know nothing. Thy will be
done. Give me thy grace.' Without that you
can do nothing.

If people do bad things, don't condemn.
Just watch. But don't you do bad things!
Just see.

*You don't need to know. Let God act
through you.*

*Let the spirit speak in you. Before you do
anything, stop and wait. Then you can act.*

*Don't give your ear to anyone. Hear only
yourself. God will speak with you.*

Don't discriminate between people.
See all alike — like you!

See God everywhere and see bliss!

There are many ways. All religions give
different ways. Follow your own path.
No one can tell you anything.

*Do your own work. I am not master of
anyone. I am only my own master.
Each is his own master. You must discover
the master in you from within.
This is the secret.*

*All are my master. I am learning from
everyone. I pick from everyone what I want
and pass on, and they too. Experience this
and you will know the truth.*

You don't want power. You want to find out the truth.

Do not care for the effects.

Difficulties come. They are a blessing!

Be like the bee which sucks honey from the flowers and then is silent.

Desire is the greatest danger. You are spirit. You don't desire anything.

Examine yourself every day – examine yourself in heart, body and mind.

Too much sleep is bad.
Too much walking, too much work is bad.
Too much anything is bad.

You must fight inside.
Fight the whole time!

You must look after the body.
Body is important.

*God must swallow you. You cannot
swallow God.*

*Do your work. Through work you can
realize God. Work for work's sake.*

*Philosophy and religion are one. Rituals and
ceremonies express philosophical truths.*

Let go the rope! Attachment is the rope.
Just go about here and there. See everything:
be a witness. Die before you die!

Impartiality – have no friends, no enemies.
That is best. Treat friends, enemies,
neighbours all alike. Don't show preference
to anyone. That is impartiality.

*Everything is in you. You don't want
to know. Let God speak in you –
otherwise there is no God. He is in you,
in me, in everyone.*

Go up and up – by thinking. Right thought,
right understanding, right observation.
Think 'I am on the top'. See all from there.

Let God give to you. Take what you want.
Reject what you don't want.

Let our bodies be worn out in
the service of others.

Middle path – no extremes.

We are all bubbles in the ocean. The bubble
is in the ocean; the ocean is in the bubble.

Think and don't think. Then later there is
no thinking – there is only spirit.

To know 'we do not know' is the final end.
When you have passed everything else,
you come to that.

Think, think, think – then you will come to 'I do not know'.

Only God is at rest, but work is going on the whole time.

By striving you can become free, but you cannot know the truth – it is beyond everything.

Pessimism is bad, optimism is good. But both are the same. Both are illusion.

God speaks in you. God thinks in you. God feels in you – in everyone.

Don't waste time. 'Time is more precious than rubies'.

True renunciation is within;
not in external show.

Tell the truth. Don't forget austerity.
Do your work. Be still.

'The kingdom of God is within you.'
Realize that within. Go deep within.

*Everything changes. The whole world up to
the highest is changing – changing the whole
time. Otherwise there would be no world.
All play!*

*You have everything. You are the whole
world. Why? Because the kingdom
of God is within you.*

Work for work's sake. Love for love's sake.

Truth is one.
Sages explain it in various ways.

It is the greatest folly to take delight in doing
what is forbidden.

God is within you, within me,
within everything. Where is God?
You cannot say where He is.

You have eyes, you have ears, you have
hands. What are you doing with them?
What is the use of eyes if you don't see?
What is the use of ears if you don't hear?

You cannot see God, you cannot hear God
– because He is everything. You cannot
know God. God knows God. He is.
But you can feel God.

There is no 'you' and 'I' and 'he'.
All are alone. There is that one thing which
is the same in all.

I do not know. You do not know.
Nobody knows.

Be still. Don't think of anything.
Let thoughts come and go.

No fear at all.

Blessings are everywhere.

Through love you can see God.

The whole world is full of truth.

The world is. But don't touch it!

The whole world is a playground.
You must play your part.

You cannot fathom God.

Up and in. Up and in.

Death is certain. There is no one
who can escape it.

All are doing work. There is no higher,
no lower.

You must open the book of the heart.
Everything is there.

Sickness plays with the body.
It cannot play with us.

Be loving!

Grow good habits, throw bad habits! But bad habits are also my friend. Bad habits come into your heart. But don't let them control you. You are the master.

Listen to the inner man. Don't be ruled by the outer. But don't divide into 'inner' and 'outer'.

Don't say 'he is great' or 'he is a bad man'.
No good, no bad. Very hard to understand.

If you live without dying, what is the use?

Every life is a question.

Keep straight. Don't go here and there.

*If you know the truth, there is no 'greater'
self or 'lower' self.*

*If you start anything, you must
go through with it.*

Every man must travel by his own path.

God is in the world. The whole world is in God.

Each is great in his own place.

*If you try to get it, it won't come. If you go
on battling direct, it won't come.
There must be surrender and
spontaneous action.*

*Everyone suffers, has pain. People have
pain in order to get benefit. Suffering means
that they are being examined for benefit.*

God is always with you – and that is the greatest news I have for you.

The heart must be pure. There is nothing more to say.